Above the Treeline

By the same author

Under Divis Mountain (2020)

Above the Treeline

Nora Hughes

Templar Poetry

Published in 2025 by Templar Poetry

Fenelon House
Kingsbridge Terrace
58 Dale Road, Matlock, Derbyshire
DE4 3NB

www.templarpoetry.com

ISBN 978-1-911132-64-6

A CIP catalogue record of this book is available from the British Library

Typeset by Pliny

Cover by Templar Design

Printed in England

ACKNOWLEDGEMENTS

Acknowledgements are due to editors of the following publications, in which versions of these poems first appeared:

Envoi, *The North*, *Poetry Worth Hearing*, *Washing Windows Too: Irish Women Write Poetry* (Arlen House).

I am grateful to Mimi Khalvati, Jane Duran and Lynne Hjelmgaard for their invaluable feedback on the manuscript, to Belinda Williams for her patience and technical wizardry, and to Bríd Keenan for sharing her knowledge of the Irish language.

I would like to thank my family, friends, fellow poets and writers, without whose insights, generosity and support this book would not have come to fruition.

ACKNOWLEDGEMENTS

for Joanna

In childhood, certain skies focused my seeing

Arthur Rimbaud

Contents

MESSAGE IN A BOTTLE

that the house held its breath
and the paving stones rang out after you

that these things were
as they were

tension in the room, rising
and falling

our childish fear, an intake of breath
and the smoking fire

those days when you sang
If I were a blackbird or

I'll take you home again Kathleen
across the ocean wide and wild

'THE PENINSULA'

The title did it, two words
and I'm longing

for the place, a scrap of land
up there in the north Atlantic.

As I search and follow
a trail of names

on a map—Milford,
Carrigart, Downings,

Trá na Rossan—
a sorrow without a name

washes over me.
I have no photos to help

or hinder, only an old poem
somewhere in the house—

but what is this sorrow?
Is it the path over the rocks

that morning, is it the sea
washing the rocks?

I see a young woman
who has lost her father

tiptoe past friends
asleep in their bunks

in the hostel, to be alone
where the Atlantic

comes in, knowing
there's no help for any of it.

HOW DEEP DOES GRIEF GO

a small stone flies
minutely, through low-lying

air, skimming the ground
what stone is this

is it basalt, bedrock
of my childhood

there it is again
a small scraping sound

A FEW GULLS, A FEW CROWS

On the road to Mathry
past the last house
we dip our toes into the dark
and push on

till our nerve fails and we turn
back to the shapes we know
around the bay, headlands
that follow us

into the house
where, in the small light
of a fire we still live by
a baby who will never be

is there again, eyes
full of the winter sea.
On the road, small sounds:
footfalls, a loose stone

scraping the tarmac.
In the dark left by a car
passing, the hill tilts:
there's a sunset

caught in the four windows
of the rented house
and in the air above the roof
a few gulls, a few crows.

THROUGH GAPS IN THE TREES

Small flares, ragged, inter-
mittent, like torches
held by a band of people

from the past: we emerge
to a tarmac road and a view
of the hospital's

boilerhouse chimney,
the tallest thing in the valley
that winds around

oval, tabletop and sugarloaf
mountains—but the chimney
is tugging me back

to the mill of my mother's
girlhood, where girls and boys
are up to their eyes

in linen down. Sheep range
over the high slopes like hail or
pebbles or the white pills

she counted out
carefully, in the morning,
on the kitchen table.

INTO THE ICY HALL I SEE HER GO

past the waiting phone, to the room
where flames sputter on the walls, shiny

with new paint for his return.
Light bends around a tin teapot,

along the arc of liquid
poured from its spout in the morning.

On a screen in the corner, reindeer
step into shadow, stretch out

their long faces: she's hungry
for the blue light of evening

in the north, where you know
the world is somewhere, something

you've been missing all along.
Muffled sounds reach her:

the dull horn of Blackstaff Mill
summoning the early shift,

a radio, a neighbour's voice.
Ahead now, among the crowd

of spinners, weavers, stitchers, doffers
gathered at the mill door, her friends

waving and calling, and the hot life
sparks up again between them.

ONE DAY AS I WALK OUT

I come upon a crowd of parents
waiting by a school gate. I search

my mother's many faces: the good
Catholic, the mill girl, the orphaned child

whose grief has no end. This morning
leaving the house I thought I heard

the noise of time, a muffled roar
ebbing and surging on the main road.

GIRL WITH YELLOW DRESS AND RIBBON

Some days she calls it 'dress',
other days she calls it 'frock'.
Every day she loves it, yellow

down to her knees, loves
her knees, her socks and shoes
on metal wheels, speeding

down Mulholland's Hill to the shop
whose name I no longer remember.
It'll come back to me, it'll all

loop around and back
to the photo I can no longer find
somewhere behind me in this room:

lips pouty, eyes puzzled,
the skin around them creased.
Her hair spouts from a ribbon

whose colour I can't be sure of
though I know it must have matched
the yellow dress, must have

streamed out behind her into
the whooshing air.

MISS DEVLIN

heads down, row on row

here is Eileen in disgrace
facing the class

her snot runs green
her ears are mucky, tears catch
on the sticky stuff
in the corners of her eyes

and here is Miss Devlin
our kind teacher, so soft, so mild

pity fights cruelty
in Miss Devlin's eyes

up and down the rows of desks
love and fear fight it out

I am a bent head
over a desk, I am not

Eileen, no
she is not me!
those tears

hanging from the crusts
in the corners of her eyes
are not mine! but am I

Miss Devlin?
is Miss Devlin
me?

Purple sky over Divis

When we were children I was cruel,
sometimes, to Jimmy M's youngest daughter—
always tagging along, cramping our style.
That changed one summer when the results
of the *Qualie* came out and a girl in our street
(who shall be nameless) hid at home
and cried, the shame too much for her,
they said. I remember a queasy
see-saw of feeling, from relief (I'm not her)
to terror (could I be her?), to pleading
over the chasm of the street, whispering
It's alright. Purple sky over Divis,
hedges dripping, my father's hand
gripped mine, soft, hard. Out of the blue,
or so it seemed, one of our neighbours,
Mrs T, spurned our friends' mother,
Mrs A, never spoke to her again, refusing
to say why, they told me. For years
Mrs T had courted Mrs A, who lived
in a big house on the front of the road.
(Mrs T is a snob, we decreed, knowing
next to nothing about it.) Mrs A retreated
behind her bay windows, double gate,
sloping garden front and back, nylon sheets—
only Mrs A could afford them,
new shade of pink, slick. Over the edge
of the twin beds we slid, head-
over-heels, screaming as the world turned
upside down. Mrs A's given name
was a spring flower, a name we called her
once it became the norm, the old
formalities abandoned. But those

11

were the days when our street boasted
an all-Ireland dancing champion,
the widow of a Stormont MP, and two
Protestant families, one of them
a few doors from us if you faced
towards the mountain: Johnny R,
handsome young brother of Billy
and Mrs R (whose given name
we never knew or I've forgotten).
Johnny was a joker, friendly
with my father, the two of them
laughing at Billy's front gate, Mrs R
a shadowy figure in the doorway.
And when, and why, did Mrs B
come into our lives? Protestant too,
home help, a big woman
towering over our frail mother,
white bun on the top of her head.
Mrs B taught us thrift, a virtue
she said, common sense, she said
and gave each child a savings book,
pages thick as cardboard, columns
of figures growing week by week
with her gift of a threepence or sixpence.
When the air in the city turned
from tense to deadly, Johnny,
Billy and Mrs R left the street
(with heavy hearts, they said). Later,
Jimmy M's young niece and her mother
died when her parents' bar, always
full of Catholics, was bombed
with the connivance of the army unit
on patrol that day, according to
eyewitness testimonies. Before he died

(of heart failure, they said), Jimmy
lived with his wife and daughters
and a son or sons I don't recall
in a house at the end of a cul-de-sac.
A narrow passage by the house
to the hill that climbs to Divis
harboured a bogeyman. Now
it harbours death: Jimmy's niece,
her mother and thirteen others
on the pages of the *Irish News*. Like I said,
when we were children I was cruel,
sometimes, to Jimmy's youngest daughter.
Not like Mrs A, who was kind, who
told me not to worry when she saw me
gagging on a mushroom vol-au-vent
she'd learned to make at boarding school,
all the rage at the time. Just spit it out,
she said, go to the bathroom and spit it out.
Ditto the time I tried to eat a chicken leg
with a knife and fork: she laughed as she bit
into the phantom chicken in her hand.
I remember on clear mornings a faint
crackle as we stepped on ice
over paving stones that last December,
my father up ahead, his winter coat
hanging off him, my mother said.
Other days, a familiar brimming
in the hedges, coal smoke, snow flurries,
more often rain or drizzle, diesel
as the bread van passed us.

TOPOGRAPHY OF A BRAIN

Someone is here with me
in the house, I am held
in a field of vision

the room irradiated
outside and inside
as in a Bonnard painting

Looking up from my book
I see Heidi
drinking her morning milk

her grandfather at the window
keeping watch as she runs
with the goats on the mountain

When bleeding began I was
puzzled, the way we are often
left bewildered

with no view other than
what pain or its absence
can tell us, or an ultra-violet

beam, or a memory, such as
Joe the breadserver reaching into his van
with a grappling pole

to hook a bap for me
Divis dark and low at the end of the street
my brain in full view now, closer

than we've ever been
The mountain has come into the room
the line between skin and air

permeable and the future
moves towards me and the past
comes back to me

A small baker's van, full
row on row
of loaves, buns, baps, 'donkeys' lugs'

Joe is floury, motherly, a warm
thing that settles in my brain
and if ever

my old fear gets hold of me
(I'm alone, no mother,
no father, Divis

unmoved), I'll summon
that figment, Joe and his bread van
on a sunny morning

'*donkey's lug*': an iced bun the size and shape of a donkey's ear.

THE LIVERPOOL BOAT
for Iris

we dock in a chilly dawn

smells of seaweed
and the ship's exhaust

cling to us   at our backs
across the water

the mothers   the fathers
the small houses

we grew up in

Sleepless, I tiptoe past the coats
snug on their hooks
in the gap below stairs
and climb the white staircase

to the yellows, browns, ochres
of the spare room: a landscape
old and vast, comes back to me,
a high plain, where sunrise

is watched from the window
of a third-class carriage
by a Belfast girl and her friends.
The train crawls over the summit

of the Meseta Central
towards the Levantine village
of the *Señora,* whose *clase*
de conversación lit up the week

all summer term: she cried
as she spoke of her loneliness
in her husband's native city—
¡Que lo quiero, lo quiero tanto!—

in a high-rise flat with a view
half-way to where the Lagan, far
from its source on a boggy hillside
drains into the Irish Sea.

Early riser

morning craves
a mother, a father, to lean in

through the rectangle of the window
I need the sun to lean in

uncertain light spreads, a drill
starts up, then a tender riff

of *Cape Town Flowers*
between birdsong and traffic hum

slips under, throwing me
off balance and for no reason

I think of the tideless sea
I haven't felt on my arms

or heard from my bed at night
since the pandemic

began: a dream, a story
told to friends, with photos

of the warm south, whose air
I can almost feel again

MARE NOSTRUM

While we sit drinking weak filter coffee
at Margaritari's after our morning swim
the sea drips off your hair

your towel, rigid with salt and sand, stiffens
on the wooden fence and you radiate
something I can't name though I soak it up

You fuss for a while about the coffee
(too bitter too strong!) then laugh
and gossip about this and that

As you dive in, the sea closes over you
and I, scrunching up my eyes
scour the silky patches on the water

till a dark head reappears, framed
between the rock the women swim out to
and the dry headland we love

'Our sea', a name given by the Romans to the Mediterranean Sea.

BAY OF ERESSOS

We pushed the twin beds together and turned off the fan
to hear waves throwing themselves on the beach

then a long low hiss as they sucked salt water through sand.
Some waves were drowned by laughter, clinking glass,

chairs scraping the floor of the taverna below. As we spoke
our words hung above the bed for a moment

before they drained away and an old song took their place,
flitting through the room, lost among the dust grains.

I recognised the shy, crooning notes that would slip
from my mother's throat those rare days when she sang

in the kitchen, though I knew very well they'd long since
flown back into the silence that swallows all sound.

MYTILINI

In the end there's no choice: we're scared
of mudslides or flash floods, but as the bad weather
sets in, to catch our flight home we leave Eressos,
heading into the mountains in heavy rain.

The streets of Mytilini are loud with traffic
but empty of refugees. There was a road sign
a while back, to the village of Moria: no mention
of a camp. I think about the Afghan boys

who came with us that summer. We picked them up
a mile or so out of Kalloní, halfway across the island.
They had walked all night from the shingle beach
on the north coast where their boat came in.

They were brothers: eighteen and seventeen,
the older boy said, leaning shyly between us.
The young one smiled and nodded, mimicking
the ra-ta-ta-ta-tat of machine gun fire

as if to account for their presence here.
Seeing the queue at the harbour, we left them
by a fountain near the municipal gardens
where a small group of men had gathered to wash.

FLIGHT A3608

there's a mountain
contained
in my porthole

turning its sharp face
away from us now

what's a mountain
for? what does this
indifference mean?

the temerity of it—
us flying, wings stiff
as no real wings are

with our portions
of penne Greek-style
and our bird's-eye view

a winged toy
throws its shadow

over the wrinkles
of the burning
Aegean

GREY MAN'S PATH

on the brae head
after the last
drystone wall

what I remember
is rock, whin
and thistle

lichens, each growing
in its own time
and in the Sea of Moyle

an island
beyond the cliff
where rough grass runs

hell-bent on
Grey Man's Path
unsought, unintended

as this *mile-a-minute*
tearing down a valley
to another sea

'*mile-a-minute*': Russian vine

23

THE CHICKENS IN HUNTER'S YARD
for Tom on his birthday

In the old photo (remember it?)
an adult hand presses my back,

holding me steady; the air
is summer-warm and the chickens

are alive, as we are alive, though you,
the youngest, have not been born:

the world is waiting for you,
you will soon appear—here you are

on my Facetime screen
all the way from California,

nice tee-shirt, coffee mug in hand.
It's mid-morning there, while here

we are entering a time of day
that leads us back to the dark.

As for the chickens in Hunter's yard,
you finally got to see them

years later, after the lost twins
who had gone to a place called *Limbo*:

you were with us on the roadside,
curly-haired, baby-faced,

giggling at the squawking rooster
and a small brown hen picking her way

through the scraps and breadcrumbs
we tossed over the floor of the yard.

RÓISÍN

I want to call up a summer—
a city street into whose cool
first-thing-in-the-morning air

we emerged, groggy
from our basement, bare-armed,
faces rapt, hurrying

through the noise and speed
of Earl's Court to the underground
scent of London

and on to Blackfriars,
to our jobs in a bookies
calculating winnings—

how we loved it
in the big smoke, in the heart
of the beast that was England!

We had just left school:
at eighteen, she was half-way
through her life

though this was hidden
from her and those who loved her
and from the English boy

enamoured of her 'Irish' looks,
her passion for film stars,
poetry and kissing—

all this I envied, maybe feared
a little, as I chafed
at the trysts in the other bed.

'Bedsit land' they called it,
street of transience, of youth
without a safety net—

no teachers, no parents, just us,
arms cool and faces hopeful,
breathing the smoggy air.

IN THE SOUTHERN NIGHT
for Deborah i.m.

stars burn with cold

sounds of friendship carry
from cafés along the bay

you were too far out

a salt wave, sudden
brings a taste

the sea took your breath

did the silent stars
call to you?

did they?

MOUSE-EAR HAWKWEED

Panicked, I push against
the weight of sand, its weight-

lessness: the merest breath
and a billion blind grains swarm

around my stem: roots
of sedge and marram grass

bind the shifting dune
as daylight moths plunder

my leaves and the wind circles—
till, in the dark, small rodents

come snuffling, rub against me:
this is the time when,

real or remembered, other worlds
reach me from the night sky.

ABHAILE

I'm going home soon, where 'home'
used to be. I'm afraid

as I was afraid in the new country, whose
strangeness moved me—

the neat houses, roads, all familiar
but I couldn't get inside.

I remember a harbour wall
open to rain and sun, dissolving

slowly, and the brown lino
that curled into the corners of the room.

'AT THE END OF MY SUFFERING'
for Geraldine i.m.

My body came back to me
acted on, cared for

a known thing—
does the mind wait

beside the operating table?
Did my soul toss and turn?

Geraldine
in her seventieth year

through the dark of her suffering
cried out for her mother

as I did that night of her death
in a dream, till dawn

encircled the yellow blind
and dark withdrew.

UNTITLED
November 2023

How can I begin
to love the world again?

The house has shrunk.
The kitchen walls contain us,

in my head we beat against them
with our fists.

What grace
eludes me? What peace?

Out of the radio, pain
pours into the room.

Look, you say, *is that
a baby snail in the lettuce?*

We watch its slow emergence
from leaf to paper bag

to worktop: a creature
fully formed, body

and shell transparent,
antennae the colour of air.

CUMHA

Hunger in the heart
is universal: its symptoms
are unmistakable

though its object may alter
in the anxious search
for the beloved.

It can be light or heavy,
a blurring
of the world's contours

or a hollowing out
of the self
that can lead to panic.

It may be soothed,
set aside, even avoided
but in life's long exile

from the beloved, be they
person, place or self,
it is rarely cured.

Tá cumha orm.

GLEANING

A high field, a dust cloud
the gulls follow, swarming

in random patterns to home in
on the husks left behind by the reaper,

a young man in a combine harvester
filling the clifftop with noise,

machine roar: as blades slice
through dry stalks, the gulls circle,

white underbellies exposed
to the gaze of walkers on the path.

But the gulls' minds are on the gleaning:
they are all focus, dive and swoop,

outstretching without pain.
There's so much we can't bear—

dark patches on the water
darker than the sea around them,

the loneliness of a father's last day,
a daughter unable to go with him

into his fear: whatever can be gleaned
from grain-dust, husks, smudges

of indigo on a bright sea,
the daughter now covets.

THE DESK JOB

After years humping sacks
in a flour mill in the city,
my father got a desk job

at Stormont: checking,
signing and binding forms
with elastic bands

till break-time when he joked
with his friend Jock
and ate the cheese sandwich

he'd made at the crack of dawn
as he waited for the fire
to blaze up and warm the house.

At his desk, under the Queen's
portrait and the latest
commands from his boss,

did he ever suffer one of his
sudden spurts of rage?
Back home, his daily practice

was to stand on the doorstep
watching the birds 'fly home'.
I sometimes caught a look

in my mother's eyes
of pain at his turned back,
his sky-gazing.

Under Divis Mountain

The walls hold back their hoard of noise, the mountain
goes dark and the birds on next door's roof strike up—

from my armchair I see a window-shaped sunset
behind my closed eyelids and you in the doorway,

thinner now, your worn jacket hanging loose.
I loved it best in winter when the room was snug

and the fire scorched our faces, before you joined
what my people called a foreign army (to save the world,

for friendship, for the wage, for all or none of these?)
Most days that hot summer of '33 I cleaned the house,

scraping at dirt that stuck to the skirting boards, chasing
dustballs across the kitchen floor. Outside, the glare

looked dangerous and the doorstep burned my feet.
I can still feel the tug of the messages on my arms

as I hauled them home and the weight of all our words,
the actions of a day, a year, a lifetime that led to this.

'the messages': 'the shopping' in twentieth-century Irish colloquial English

COUNTDOWN

Before we met, the daughter made a firm decision, she later told me, to give up words. She was referring to her passion for word searches, word ladders, crosswords, words-within-words and—most addictive of all—words hidden in the registrations of cars and other vehicles.

What you must do, her friends advised, is every time a well-known pattern pops up push it gently away. She had been practising this for some time, ever since the day, about six months after her mother's death (she was on her bike, panniers bulging with the weekly shop), when suddenly the street narrowed and the car bumpers lining the pavements swelled up, pushing their letters and numbers at her.

The origin of this, she mused, must lie in her weekly visits in the final year, when they would watch Countdown together, trays of tea and toasted soda bread on their laps. Often, she confessed, she would take her eyes off the ticking clock or the conundrum for a moment to catch with glee the sight of yellow butter running.

THE SHADOW ON THE HILL

grows longer, it swallows
the grazing sheep one by one,

the run-down farmhouse,
its stricken sheepdog's bark

carrying over the valley
to where we stand and watch.

Under a half-moon, the bay
fills slowly: car lights

sweep the headland, pick out
an unlit cottage, let it go.

I am searching the water
for the flat black rock

where yesterday a mother seal
basked with her restless young.

WHO IS THIS?

Who is this old woman repeating *croissant croissant*,
a mouthful of sounds she's never made

in her life before. I'm amazed, I who assumed
she'd barely manage the trills, nasals and gutterals

she's forming now, an *r* rolling in her throat,
an *n* glottal against her tongue: this is not

the mother I remember, on her knees, face smudged
with soot, struggling to get a fire going

for the new friend I'd brought home from school.
Her new friend is her wheelchair! Far better

than hobbling breathless across a room.
In the car one morning on an outing somewhere

off the North Circular, as we inch along
a packed slip road, she bursts out *I love this!*

She is ninety years old, her death is not far off,
all her life she has been terrified

and we are driving onto an ugly six-lane highway
and she is full of joy.

Red sky at night

Such a scene before our eyes! The sky aglow,
the Pope on a wall behind us blessing the house
while the parents' bed in its iron frame holds steady.
We look out past the Lucozade factory chimney

to the unseen mills of the city, and the Falls Road
burning, as we always knew it would, had learned
to expect. At twenty, I begin to know the meaning
of a red sky, watched from a bedroom window,

mother and daughter side by side, like the friends
we seldom were, those years when our worlds
and our ways collided. She's a little taller still—

a childhood illness slowed my early growth
in that other time of danger, when they took turns
to sit with me all night, nursed me, saved me.

Rathlin

I wear my new dress stiffly, like a stranger
as we're shepherded onto the ferry.
The sea's quiet so we huddle together

on deck, watching the lighthouse
come closer and move further away
till we're in the harbour. All afternoon

the sun beams down as we bump
over fields in a tractor (were there
no cars, no roads, on the island?).

But on the journey back the sky
turns thick, dark and a high wind
tosses the boat around like a skittle.

All this stayed with me, crystal-clear
over the years, but for something
I lost sight of, till a chance remark

by one of the McKinleys, whose cousins
we visited on the island, brought it back.
"Lord, that storm was a bad one!"

What came to me then as I re-lived
the wind's attack (the sea in my mouth
and the mad see-sawing of the boat)

was my mother, turned essence-of-mother,
mountainous, holding me to her chest.

ABUELO

De niños, no sabíamos que lo fusilaron
que murió allí en la calle
en la piedra de la calle
rodeado de caras y ojos
de mujeres y hombres para quienes
era enemigo

Nos dijeron que murió de un infarto
que se le falló el corazón
su corazón de padre
padre de mi padre
padre de nuestro querido tío
padre de tía y tíos exiliados, desconocidos

Se le falló el corazón de nunca-a-ser
abuelo

GRANDA

As children, we didn't know they'd shot him
that he died there in the street
on the stone of the street
surrounded by faces and eyes
of women and men for whom
he was an enemy

They told us he died of a heart attack
that his heart failed him
his father's heart
father of my father
father of our beloved uncle
father of aunt and uncles exiled and unknown

His never-to-be
grandfather's heart failed him

THE PAINTING IN THE SITTING ROOM

Green, a total feeling of green,
a green so calm, so blessed
I could barely imagine
such a place: a copy

someone said, of a postcard,
a rural scene whose only
detail I remember is the arc
of a bridge above a river.

Uncle Leo, the artist,
was said to be musical
and played the violin
('violin' not 'fiddle'

he and Tillie called it).
She accompanied him
on her mandolin,
they played duets together

though what tunes I don't know
nor why they gave us
that one-and-only recital
in this very room.

When Tillie married Leo
they were both well
into their fifties and Leo,
in the gossips' version

of his story, invalided out
of a job in the shipyard,
was on the lookout
for 'somewhere to light'.

'MS' was whispered
to explain the trembling
and the nodding
of his head as he played.

THE BOXROOM

I wake in the high, narrow bed
of my brother's childhood

in the boxroom that smells of dust
and clean sheets. His toy soldiers,

meticulously painted, arrayed
in ranks on the bookcase,

reach forward, bayonets fixed.
On my eyelids is the imprint

of a mountain, a street
and the shine of privet hedge.

KITCHEN SONG
for Mary

I'm awake half the night, till at last
sleep finds me. I see

two girls, one dark, one fair,
hair plaited and beribboned—

when their time comes
and courage is needed

will they find it? Our mother
believed she couldn't sing, but tonight

those timid, wobbly notes
that reached us from the kitchen

are pushing into the walls
of my dream.

On the Marshes

The light today, almost white
after weeks of drought, seems to pour

over the reeds and purple seed-heads.
In a month of rain, gulls

gathered on the lake that was
this meadow; when heat came,

baking the spongy paths
till they cracked, everything green

flourished. We're up to our knees
in swaying grass, me and the other

older woman approaching
on the track. Seeing me

break into an eager spurt, then stop
to follow a ladder of vetch

through a reedbed, she lets out
a bellowing laugh.

No slacking! she yells
and for a while we stand there

facing each other
laughing and marvelling.

Don't you love all this green?
The way the grass sways!

Speech sounds reach me from the gravel path

Glides, clicks, plosives, gutturals
launch themselves across the water
that lines this urban marsh, sailing over
unruly grass and vetch that burrows
through reedbeds, over baked walkways

past the lonely blue of the boathouse
into the threads of green algae
combed through water by the synchronised
pulling and straining of the rowers.
Word-streams, like and unlike my own

outpourings and withholdings,
in tongues like and unlike my own,
pass through me, their meanings sensed
or not: these strangers, fellow-talkers,
have settled here, as I have, till our words

people the parklands. Something almost
like kinship can be sensed among
us and the banded cattle transplanted
to the marshes to tame the marauding
docks, comfreys and Michaelmas daisies,

their broad, striped backs loved
and loved again as we pause our talk
to hear a low sound: blow-ins tearing
as they're ripped from the ground, to be
chewed, liquidised and ruminated on.

Algae

what I have been
is my life, and now in the glaze
of a frozen waterway

algae, the brighter the green, the uglier
they're thought to be

once as a schoolgirl I sensed
the ill-will of a teacher, magnified
in my child's eye

and the fear
of what she thought she saw in me

bloomed in the ice between us

LAMENT
for Eve i.m.

for one whose grief burned
as anger, whose words spiked

in the mouth and on the page
whose longing scoured the faces

of friends while the pills
on the kitchen table went astray

whose thoughts sparked
and cavorted through notebooks

whose talk thrummed in the cafés
and on the marshes

who waited with me
to listen to a crack willow that leans

over the water, whose
view of trees from her room

in a care home stopped

BRUSHED COTTON

I listen to the silence of the bedside clock with its sweeping
mechanism: no tick, no false promise of minutes, seconds or
nanoseconds. At 1.30 pm (give or take a minute, an hour or
an afternoon), the Consultant will probe the white mound
and its dark companion in the recess of the body where they
lie together under a lamp held steady by her young assistant.
In the spare room where I've migrated to see out the night,
the desk emits not one but two blue beams. *Turn off all devices*,
urge the sleep gurus. But the halo around the window (thanks
to a merciless neighbour's fear of the dark) radiates LED light.
I hug the hot water bottle, stroke its cloth cover (home-made
to soften the bottle's rubber ridges by one who lies downstairs
in the double bed: with any luck the blackout blind will do its
work and let her sleep till morning). Up here, where there's
no morning, I breathe in and out, in and out. *There's no such
thing as minutes, seconds or nanoseconds*, says the hand as it circles
the clock face.

The Neurologist and the Radiographer

introduced themselves, said *Relax*
and invited me to watch the film
to be projected on a screen
to my left. The Neurologist began
by making a small opening:
an X-ray camera guided us
past my beating heart on our way
to the brain. The Radiographer
moved in closer, hovering
above a flood plain traversed
by a scarlet network. As I gazed
at its rivers and tributaries,
the Neurologist searched
for the breach where the spillage
had occurred, pausing to examine
every kink and bend in the flow—
till a small tear, not far
from the *pia mater*, revealed itself.
The Radiographer and I looked on
as she scanned the terrain for any
tell-tale bulge or build-up,
then the camera led us back
through my body to the frozen
open groin, which the Neurologist
sealed with half-a-dozen stitches.
At a signal between them,
the film ended and they both
offered me their congratulations.

'pia mater' ('tender mother'): protective membrane surrounding the brain

Risk

These eyes
I look into
hold mine
obstinate
as the weeds
spreading now
through the garden
and the overhanging
espaliered rose
that shocks
in its abundance
Not to risk
is like a slow
drying out
a kind of
lonely exile
while
the soft body
ages

NIGHT-TIME

I watch her scramble into bed,
tug an old white tee-shirt
up over her head, take aim.

I follow its brief flight through air
past the chest of drawers, the blue-
curtained window, to the heap

on her grandmother's chair
where it comes to land—
how to match such theatre?

My own way is slow, full of
night thoughts in the borderland
between the lived day and its end—

layer by layer, still warm,
old favourites peel away (hooded
jumper, vest of midnight blue).

I feel them graze my neck,
ears, temples, and as they drop
and settle, let night come close.

Breakfast at La Duchesse

rough-eyed after the night
you'll squint   your half-awake
squint   your rumpled cheek

and if it rains   we'll make a dash
for it   and fling ourselves
at a table near the door

THE VISIT

sometimes
you arrive
the way

night falls
into the long
summer day

its slow
headlong descent
through the pores

of evening
to where the heart
holds on tight

holds its hunger
tight
but the heart too

is porous
and in no time
I am awash

SMALL AND PURPLE AT THE EDGE OF THINGS

They keep on flowering,
ignoring the facts of winter, of frost

on early spring mornings as I dip
and sweep through my *qi gong* routine,

catching my peripheral vision.
They don't cooperate: no seasonal

sweetness brought to light, for I'm
no great gardener. They lay ambush

as I descend through a skyful
of blackbirds, crows, a passing plane,

and down into that corner of the patio
where small purple stars lurk.

LARCH

Every evening after dinner they set out in the near dark
to visit the larch tree at the end of the lane.
Nothing much happened:

an evening bird, their footfalls
tinny on the empty road, larch branches
sweeping up a wind.

They would stand in its presence a while as it gathered
what was left of the day into itself.
Then one of them would turn

and they would face towards the house again—
slits of light under the door,
around the window with the broken blind

and they would find themselves, for a moment, somewhere
between the soul of the house
and the soul of the tree behind them.

ABOVE THE TREELINE

the mountain hums
come back

into the house, bring
the air in with you

bring the mountain

NOTES

'THE PENINSULA'
Seamus Heaney in *Door into the Dark* (1969)

PURPLE SKY OVER DIVIS
'the *Qualie*': Qualifying Examination (Eleven Plus).

'Jimmy's young niece and her mother...' In December 1971
a loyalist group, the Ulster Volunteer Force (UVF), planted
a bomb at McGurk's Bar in Belfast, killing 15 people. Eye-
witness testimonies, together with documentary evidence
released years later, point to collusion by the British military
authorities.

TOPOGRAPHY OF A BRAIN
'I am held/in a field of vision/the room irradiated/outside
and inside...'. During an *angiogram* (diagnostic X-ray proce-
dure), a camera is inserted into the body.

IF ON A WINTER'S NIGHT A TRAVELLER...
Italo Calvino, *Se una notte d'inverno un viaggiatore* (1979)

'clase/de conversación': conversation class
'¡Que lo quiero, lo quiero tanto!': I love him, I love him so much!

EARLY RISER
Cape Town Flowers: jazz album, Abdullah Ibrahim (1997)

GREY MAN'S PATH
'Grey Man's Path': a fissure in the cliff face on the North
Antrim coast.

ABHAILE
ABHAILE (pronounced *AWÆLLA* in Ulster Irish): *home, homewards*

'AT THE END OF MY SUFFERING'
From the title poem of "The Wild Iris", Louise Glück (1992)

CUMHA
(pronounced COO-EE *in Ulster Irish*): *loneliness, homesickness, parting sorrow*
(Ó Dónaill's Irish-English Dictionary/*teangleann.ie*)

'*Tá cumha orm*' (TA COO-EE ORUM): literally '*Loneliness is on me*'

RED SKY AT NIGHT
In August 1969, loyalist paramilitaries invaded the Falls Road. Many people were burned out of their homes.

ABUELO/GRANDA
I wrote this poem in Spanish before translating it into English, a process inspired by Jhumpa Lahiri's book *In Other Words*, in which texts in Italian are followed by versions in English. Lahiri's mother tongue is Bengali and she grew up in the US speaking English, but for a while she wrote in Italian, after studying the language for some years. She says: 'In Italian I write without style, in a primitive way. I'm always uncertain.' To explore this idea, I wrote *Abuelo* and *Granda*.

SPEECH SOUNDS REACH ME FROM THE GRAVEL PATH
'blow-ins': in Ireland refers to people who have moved to a place where they have no roots